The Best 50

STRAWBER

RECIPES

Joanna White

Bristol Publishing Enterprises
Hayward, California

ISBN-13: 978-1-55867-340-3
ISBN-10: 1-55867-340-7

Printed in the United States of America.

Cover design: Frank J. Paredes
Cover photography: John A. Benson
Food stylist: Randy Mon

STRAWBERRIES: ADAPTABLE FRUIT OF THE HEART

Strawberries are one of the most delicious and nutritious fruits. They are sodium-free, cholesterol-free, fat-free and low in calories. Strawberries are a recognized source of potassium, folic acid, vitamin C and dietary fiber. They are one of the few sources, along with grapes and cherries, of ellagic acid, a compound which has been shown to prevent carcinogens from turning healthy cells into cancerous ones in cell cultures and lab animals. Strawberries are incredibly adaptable—this book contains recipes for Breakfast Foods, Appetizers, Drinks, Entrees and Desserts. These versatile berries are soft, succulent and seductive!

PURCHASING AND STORING STRAWBERRIES

1. Look for evenly colored, plump berries with fresh green leaves.

2. Strawberries are highly perishable and should be used within a

day or two of purchase.

3. To store strawberries, cover and store them unwashed in the refrigerator—do not crowd or press.

4. If any of the berries are moldy, remove them immediately to prevent the mold from spreading.

5. Wash and hull berries just before using otherwise they will soften and mold faster. A salad spinner works well for removing excess water from berries.

6. Strawberries may be frozen whole or in pieces. To freeze, wash and hull, sprinkle with sugar, and toss gently with your hands. Place in freezer containers or zip-lock bags. Use within 1 year.

7. If you wish to maintain the shape of the berry, wash berries in cold water, hull and place on flat trays in a single layer (well spaced out) and freeze.

When berries are frozen hard, transfer berries to freezer containers or freezer bags (removing as much air as possible).

STRAWBERRY MEASUREMENT EQUIVALENTS

- 1 quart weighs 1¼ to 1½ lb. and yields 4 to 5 servings.
- 8 quarts weighs 12 pounds and makes 13 pints frozen.
- 6 cups (or 1½ quarts) is needed for a 9-inch pie.
- 1 cup sliced fresh berries equals a 10 oz. pkg. frozen berries.
- Add a sprinkling of black pepper to puréed strawberries to enhance the flavor.
- 1 pint strawberries equals: about 12 large or 36 small berries
  3¼ cups whole berries
  2¼ cups sliced berries
  1⅔ cups puréed berries

STRAWBERRY NUTRITION INFORMATION

All nutrition information based on 1 cup (8 to 10) fresh strawberries:

- Calories: about 50
- Protein: 1 g
- Fat: 0.6 g
- Carbohydrates: 11 g

- Sugar: 7 g
- Fiber: 3.5 g
- Iron: 0.6 mg
- Sodium: 2 mg
- Calcium: 22 mg
- Phosphate: 30 mg
- Riboflavin: 0.1 mg

- Vitamin C: 85 mg
- Potassium: 240 mg
- Zinc: 0.2 mg
- Niacin: 0.4 mg
- Vitamin: B6 92 mcg
- Folate: 34 mcg

HEALTH INFORMATION

Apart from the obvious health benefits, a recent study by Dr. Gene Spiller, Nutrition and Health Research Center, has shown that eating one serving (about 8 to 10 strawberries) a day can significantly decrease blood pressure, which may reduce the risk of heart disease. Other studies show additional benefits: Strawberries are found to reduce risk of cancer, rheumatoid arthritis and enhance memory function.

STRAWBERRY COFFEE CAKE

Servings: 6

Coffee cake is a popular breakfast treat. For a change, use a combination of berries, mixing strawberries with other berries like blackberries and blueberries.

2 cups all-purpose flour	1/3 cup milk
2 tsp. baking powder	1 1/2 cups fresh strawberries
1/2 cup sugar	3 tbs. butter
1/3 cup butter	1/4 cup sugar
1 large egg, beaten	3 tbs. flour

Preheat oven to 400°. Sift flour, baking powder and sugar together. Cut in 1/3 cup butter into flour mixture with a pastry blender. Combine egg and milk and add to dry ingredients, blending thoroughly. Grease an 8-x-8-inch pan and spread mixture in pan. Cover dough with strawberries. In a small bowl, combine remaining ingredients with pastry blender until crumbly. Sprinkle this mixture on top of the strawberries. Bake for 25 minutes and serve warm.

STRAWBERRY SCONES

Makes: 8–12

Whenever possible I try to use freezer jam because it imparts a really fresh homemade flavor. This is my favorite scone recipe made with cream which makes the scones extremely flaky. Strawberry Butter, *page 7, and* Enhanced Strawberry Jam, *page 7, give a double blast of flavor.*

1¾ cup flour
2 tsp. baking powder
1 tbs. sugar
½ tsp. salt

¼ cup cold butter
2 large eggs, beaten
⅓ cup cream
1–2 tbs. sugar (for sprinkling)

In a bowl, sift flour, baking powder, sugar and salt together. Cut butter into pieces and use a pastry blender until butter pieces are the size of peas. In another bowl, beat eggs and reserve 2 tbs. of beaten egg for glaze. Beat remaining eggs with cream and add to flour mixture, combining with a few swift strokes.

Divide dough in half and just barely press dough together. Press the dough out on a floured board, mounding the dough in the center. Cut dough rounds into either 4 or 6 wedges (depending on the desired size). Place wedges on a buttered baking sheet, brush with reserved glaze and sprinkle with sugar. Bake scones at 450° for 15 minutes or until slightly brown. Partially slice scone open and serve hot with flavored butter and jam.

STRAWBERRY BUTTER
$\frac{1}{2}$ lb. butter, softened
$\frac{1}{2}$ cup strawberry jam

Beat butter and jam together in a mixer and spread on hot scones.

ENHANCED STRAWBERRY JAM
1 cup strawberry jam, prefer freezer variety
$\frac{1}{2}$ cup finely chopped fresh strawberries

In a bowl, combine jam and fresh strawberries. Serve on strawberry-flavored buttered scones.

STRAWBERRY STUFFED FRENCH TOAST

Serve this delicious French toast with Strawberry Syrup, *page 18,* Strawberry Sauce, *page 53, or pure maple syrup. Frozen strawberries can be substituted (but drain thoroughly and add more sugar if necessary).*

8 oz. cream cheese, softened
2-3 tbs. sugar
1 cup chopped fresh strawberries
12 slices of day-old brioche or sourdough bread
4 large eggs, beaten
3/4 cup half-and-half
3 tbs. sugar
1/2 tsp. pure vanilla extract
dash of salt

In a bowl, beat cream cheese and sugar together until well mixed. Add strawberries and just barely mix to combine.

Spread cream cheese mixture over 6 slices of bread and top with remaining bread slices. In a bowl, combine eggs, half-and-half, sugar, vanilla and salt.

Preheat oven to 425° and grease a baking sheet. Dip sandwiches in egg mixture and place on baking sheet. Baste the top of the sandwiches with remaining egg mixture. Bake for 15 minutes, or until golden brown, turning sandwiches once half way through the baking process. Serve immediately.

STRAWBERRY CHEESE BLINTZES

Servings: 6

Serve with sausage, bacon or ham and fresh orange juice.

CREPE BATTER

3 large eggs
¾ cup milk
½ cup water
1 tsp. salt

1 tsp. baking powder
1 cup flour
3 tbs. melted butter
extra butter for frying

Combine eggs, milk, and water in a food processor workbowl or blender container and process for 1 minute. Add remaining ingredients and process until smooth. Sieve through a strainer and allow mixture to set for 30 minutes before frying. Heat a crepe pan with a dab of butter and fry crepes ahead of time.

BLINTZ FILLING

16 oz. cream cheese, softened
1 cup dry cottage cheese
1 cup ricotta cheese (whole
   milk if available)

2 large eggs
pinch of salt
3 tbs. sugar
melted butter for brushing

In a mixer or food processor, beat cream cheese until soft and creamy. Add dry cottage cheese and ricotta cheese and beat well. Then add remaining ingredients and beat until well mixed.

Preheat oven to 350°. Fill each crepe with 2 tbs. of filling. Fold crepes into squares and place on a buttered baking sheet. Brush with melted butter and bake for 10 to 15 minutes until crepe bundles become puffy. Serve with sour cream topping and *Strawberry Sauce,* page 53.

BLINTZ TOPPING

1 cup sour cream
2 tbs. brown sugar
2 tbs. orange juice

10 oz. frozen strawberries,
    thawed
sugar to taste
few drops lemon juice

In a bowl, combine sour cream, brown sugar and orange juice. In a food processor workbowl or blender container, blend berries, sugar and lemon juice together. Taste and determine if you wish to add more sugar or lemon juice.

STRAWBERRY BREAD

Serve with softened cream cheese mixed with chopped straw-berries sweetened to your liking.

2/3 cup vegetable oil or melted
   butter
2 large eggs
1 1/3 cups mashed strawberries
3/4 cup sugar

1 3/4 cups all-purpose flour
2 tsp. cinnamon
1/2 tsp. baking soda
1/2 tsp. salt
3/4 cup chopped walnuts or pecans

Preheat oven to 350°. Prepare an 8-inch loaf pan by cutting a piece of brown paper to line the bottom of pan. Grease paper and side of pan with butter or butter flavored cooking spray. In a mixer, beat together oil, eggs and strawberries until blended. Add remaining ingredients and blend until well mixed. Pour mixture into prepared loaf pan and bake for 1 hour or until a knife inserted in the center comes out clean. Allow bread to cool in pan before removing.

BREAKFAST EGG BAKE

If desired, serve this with a dollop of sour cream, vanilla yogurt or sweetened whipped cream.

4 cups fresh strawberries, sliced
1/3 cup sugar, or to taste
4 tbs. butter
6 large eggs
3 cups milk

1 1/2 cups all-purpose flour
2/3 cup sugar
1/2 tsp. salt
1/2 tsp. pure vanilla extract

In a bowl, combine strawberries with sugar. Allow mixture to release its juice while preparing and baking egg mixture. Heat oven to 375°. Place butter in a 9-x-13-inch glass or ceramic pan and set in oven while making egg mixture. In a mixer, beat eggs and milk together and add remaining ingredients (excluding strawberry mixture). Swirl melted butter in glass pan to coat bottom and sides. Pour egg mixture into dish and bake for about 30 to 35 minutes, or until golden brown. Serve immediately with sweetened strawberries.

STRAWBERRY WALNUT MUFFINS

For a change, I also make this recipe using a combination of chopped fresh rhubarb and strawberries. Another alternative is to add ¹/₂ cup white chocolate chips to this recipe.

1¹/₂ cups flour
³/₄ cup sugar
¹/₂ tsp. baking soda
¹/₂ tsp. salt
1 large egg, beaten
¹/₂ cup buttermilk or sour milk
¹/₃ cup vegetable oil or melted butter
1 tsp. pure vanilla or strawberry extract
1 cup chopped strawberries
¹/₂ cup chopped toasted walnuts

WALNUT TOPPING
1/2 cup brown sugar
1/3 cup chopped walnuts
1/2 tsp. cinnamon

Preheat oven to 325°. In a bowl, combine all dry ingredients. Then add egg, buttermilk, oil and vanilla or strawberry extract and stir just enough to blend together. Fold in strawberries and walnuts. Spray muffin tins with butter flavored cooking spray. Fill muffin tins.

In another bowl, combine topping ingredients and sprinkle on top of muffin dough. Bake for 25 minutes. Muffins are very tender; allow the muffins to cool in the tin before removing.

DUTCH BABIES

A Dutch baby is a large German puffy pancake that is baked in a very hot oven. Normally it is served with apples and lemon juice, but fresh strawberries take it to another level. If desired, serve with strawberry syrup or sweetened whipped cream.

1/2 cup flour
2 tbs. sugar
1/2 tsp. salt
2 large eggs
2/3 cup half-and-half
1 tsp. pure vanilla extract
2 tbs. butter
3/4 cup thickly-sliced
  strawberries, washed and
  hulled

2 tbs. brown sugar
1/4 tsp. cinnamon
1 tsp. fresh lemon juice
dusting of powdered sugar for
  garnish

Preheat oven to 500°. In a medium bowl, combine flour, sugar and salt. In a small bowl, whisk eggs, half-and-half and vanilla together. Stir this into dry ingredients until no lumps remain.

Heat butter on medium-high in a 9- to 10-inch nonstick, oven-proof skillet until butter is sizzling. Pour batter into hot skillet and immediately place skillet in oven and reduce heat to 425°. Bake for about 18 minutes, until pancake is puffy and edges are brown. In a bowl, combine strawberries, brown sugar, cinnamon and lemon juice. Remove skillet from oven, transfer Dutch Baby to serving plate. Serve immediately with sweetened strawberries on top and a dusting of powdered sugar.

STRAWBERRY SYRUP

Serve this freshly made syrup with waffles, pancakes, or French toast. Another possibility is to use this recipe to sweeten smoothies and shakes or serve over ice cream.

1 lb. sliced strawberries	pinch of salt
½ cup sugar	2 tbs. fresh lemon juice
½ cup water	a few drops of pure strawberry
⅓ cup light corn syrup	extract, optional

In a large saucepan, bring strawberries, sugar, water, corn syrup and salt to a boil over medium-high heat. Stir until sugar dissolves. Allow mixture to boil, uncovered, for about 10 minutes, stirring occasionally. Remove sauce from heat and stir in lemon juice, then strain mixture through a sieve. Taste and determine if you wish to add strawberry extract. Chill until ready to serve.

Note: Pure strawberry extract is often available in health food stores.

PIQUANT STRAWBERRY PRESERVES

Makes: 3 cups

This recipe can be used as a sweet or savory condiment. As an appetizer, consider serving this with goat cheese on toasted bread rounds.

3 cups fresh strawberries (washed, hulled and sliced into quarters)
2$\frac{1}{4}$ cups sugar
4$\frac{1}{2}$ tbs. balsamic vinegar
4$\frac{1}{2}$ tbs. water
1 tsp. cracked black pepper

Place all ingredients in a heavy saucepan and stir to combine. Bring mixture to a boil, then reduce to a simmer and cook for about 15 minutes or until mixture becomes thick and translucent. Cool, cover and chill until ready to use.

Note: Mixture will last about 3 weeks in refrigerator.

STRAWBERRY SALSA

Makes: 2½–3 cups

Serve this with crisp tortilla chips. For a change, try adding some chopped avocado to the salsa just before serving.

1–2 jalapeño peppers, stemmed, seeded and finely chopped
2½ cups finely chopped fresh strawberries
½ cup finely chopped sweet or white onions
¼ cup finely chopped cilantro
1½ tsp. fresh lime juice
1 tsp. sugar
½ tsp. salt, or more to taste

Use gloves to prepare jalapeños. Be careful not to touch your eyes or face. Start out with 1 jalapeño and mix all ingredients together, taste and determine if you wish to add the remaining jalapeño.

BERRY AND NUT BRIE

Brie cheese goes well with fruit and is incredibly versatile. For a variation, consider using a combination of mixed berries—including strawberries—that are partially mashed. Serve with small bread rounds or crackers.

1 small wheel of brie
1 cup chopped strawberries, washed and hulled
sprinkling of granulated sugar or brown sugar
$1/2$ cup lightly chopped, slivered toasted almonds
a few fresh strawberries for garnish

Preheat oven to 350°. Place brie on baking sheet and heat in oven for about 10 to 15 minutes, until soft. Meanwhile, place strawberries in a bowl and sprinkle sugar to taste over strawberries. Remove cheese from oven and carefully remove top of rind. Cover with sweetened berries and sprinkle with toasted nuts.

GINGER BERRY CHUTNEY

As an appetizer, serve this flavorful spread with softened cream cheese and crackers. As a dessert, mix with slightly sweetened cream cheese or whipped cream along with a crisp cookie.

½ cup golden raisins
½ cup orange juice
½ cup brown sugar, packed
½ cup *Strawberry Wine Vinegar,* page 23
½ cup strawberry jam

1 tbs. minced fresh ginger
1 orange, peeled, seeded and chopped
4 cups chopped strawberries
½ cup slivered toasted almonds, lightly chopped

In a large, non-reactive saucepan, combine raisins, orange juice, brown sugar, vinegar, jam, ginger and chopped orange. Cook on medium heat for 15 minutes, stirring frequently. Add strawberries, reduce heat and simmer for 10 minutes longer, stirring occasionally. Remove pan from heat and add almonds. Allow mixture to cool, then cover and refrigerate until ready to use.

STRAWBERRY WINE VINEGAR

Makes: 2 cups

Make your own strawberry wine vinegar at home for use on fruits, salads or in vinaigrette. The vinegar keeps in a dark, cool place indefinitely.

1 pt. sliced strawberries, hulled
2 cups white wine vinegar
2 tbs. sugar

In a bowl, stir together the strawberries, vinegar and sugar and let the mixture stand, covered, at room temperature for 2 days.

Discard the strawberries with a slotted spoon and strain the vinegar through a fine sieve lined with a triple thickness of rinsed and squeezed cheesecloth into a bowl. Transfer vinegar to a bottle with a tight-fitting lid and use in salad dressings and marinades.

VEGGIE AND STRAWBERRY DIP

Makes: about 1 qt.

Serve with crispy tortilla chips, savory crackers or crusty bread. I prefer to use English cucumbers because they are seedless and "burpless".

1 large English cucumber, peeled and finely chopped
1–2 green onions, finely chopped
1 yellow pepper, seeded and diced
1 1/2 tbs. chopped fresh cilantro
1/4 cup seasoned rice vinegar
black pepper to taste
2 cups fresh strawberries, washed, hulled and chopped

In a medium bowl, combine all ingredients except strawberries. Cover and refrigerate for at least 1 hour. Just before serving, add strawberries then taste and adjust seasonings.

CREAMY STRAWBERRY DIP

Makes: 3 cups

Serve this creamy delight with fresh fruit such as pineapple, strawberries, bananas and melons. I usually serve a bowl of chopped toasted walnuts or almonds and/or granola alongside for guests who desire some "crunch".

1½ cups chopped strawberries, washed and hulled
one 8 oz. pkg. cream cheese, softened
1 cup sour cream
¼ cup packed brown sugar
2 tbs. fresh lemon juice
garnish with fresh whole berries

In a food processor workbowl or blender container, process strawberries until puréed. Add remaining ingredients and process until smooth. Transfer to a serving dish, cover and chill until ready to serve.

CRANBERRY STRAWBERRY SAUCE

Makes: 4 cups

This sauce can be served alongside cold meats, bread and soften creamed cheese. It can also be used as a dipping sauce for cooked and cubed poultry.

two 10 oz. pkg. frozen
  strawberries, thawed
1/2 cup sugar
1/3 cup water
one 12 oz. pkg. cranberries

2 tbs. finely chopped
  crystallized ginger
1 tbs. orange zest
two 4-inch pieces cinnamon
  sticks

Drain juice from thawed strawberries into large saucepan, reserving berries for later. Add sugar and water, cook on medium-high stirring constantly until sugar dissolves. Add cranberries, ginger, orange zest and cinnamon sticks. Simmer for 10 minutes, stirring occasionally. Stir in reserved strawberries and remove from heat. Remove cinnamon sticks and discard; taste and adjust sweetness if desired. Cool, cover and refrigerate until ready to serve.

STRAWBERRY DAIQUIRI

This is a potent daiquiri that is quick to fix and delicious. Garnish edge of glass with a fresh strawberry.

1 lb. pkg. whole, unsweetened frozen strawberries, unthawed
1 cup coconut cream
$\frac{1}{4}$ cup fresh lemon juice
$\frac{1}{4}$ cup grenadine syrup
1 cup light rum

Place all ingredients in a food processor workbowl or blender container and blend until smooth.

Taste and determine if you wish to add more rum or coconut cream to your personal preference.

ULTIMATE STRAWBERRY SHAKE

Servings: 2

Multiple strawberry ingredients create a delicious and refreshing drink that can be made richer depending on the fat-content of the milk used.

2 cups milk (skim, 2%, or whole)
2 cups strawberry sorbet
1 cup hulled and sliced strawberries
2 tbs. strawberry jam, prefer freezer jam
1 cup crushed ice

Combine all ingredient in a blender container and blend until thick and smooth.

STRAWBERRY SMOOTHIE

Smoothies are generally a mixture of fruit, juice and ice. A touch of lemon juice creates a fresher flavor.

1 small banana, peeled and cut into small pieces
1³/₄ cups sliced strawberries, washed and hulled
¹/₃ cup milk, soy milk or kefir
¹/₃ cup apple juice, cranberry juice or white grape juice
1 tbs. sugar or honey, or more to taste
¹/₂ cup crushed ice
dash of fresh lemon juice, optional

Place banana pieces and sliced strawberries on a baking sheet and set in freezer for about 15 minutes. Combine all ingredients in a food processor workbowl or blender container and process until smooth. Taste and determine if you wish to add more sugar or lemon juice.

AGUA FRESCA

This Mexican favorite is thirst-quenching and colorful. The high proportion of water makes this drink refreshing rather than filling. Depending on the sweetness of the berries, adjust amount of sugar added.

4½ cups fresh sliced strawberries
⅓–½ cup sugar, or to taste
3 tbs. lime juice
5 cups cold water

In a food processor or blender, process all the ingredients, using the least amount of sugar to start. Taste and determine if you wish to add more sugar. If the drink is too sweet, increase the amount of lime juice. Strain the drink through a sieve and refrigerate until ready to serve.

CHILLED STRAWBERRY SOUP

Servings: 4

This is a delightful starter dish or a refreshing luncheon entrée. Serve with tea sandwiches and crunchy vegetables or vegetable salad.

1 lb. frozen strawberries, thawed
1 cup half-and-half
1 cup sour cream
$\frac{1}{2}$ cup sugar, or to taste
2 tbs. white wine, prefer sweet variety
a dollop of whipped cream, a whole strawberry and mint leaves
  for garnish.

In a food processor workbowl or blender container, purée strawberries and add remaining ingredients, except garnish. Chill at least 4 hours before serving.

STRAWBERRY SALAD
WITH POPPY SEED DRESSING

This popular salad is a hit with everyone. Serve with a crusty bread or sweet bread such as Hawaiian bread rolls found in most supermarkets.

4 cups chopped mixed salad greens
1 small sweet onion or red onion, thinly sliced
1 can mandarin oranges, drained
1 pt. sliced strawberries, washed and hulled
3/4 cup sugar
1 tsp. mustard powder
1 tsp. salt
1/3 cup apple cider vinegar
2 tsp. chopped scallions
1 cup vegetable oil
2 tsp. poppy seeds

Divide salad greens between 4 individual plates. Top with sliced onion, mandarin oranges and strawberries.

To make dressing, combine sugar, mustard powder, salt, vinegar and scallions in a food processor workbowl or blender container and process to mix. With the machine running, slowly drizzle in the oil. Stir in the poppy seeds. Taste and adjust flavor if needed.

Pour dressing on greens just before serving.

GRAPES AND STRAWBERRY
MEDLEY SALAD

Makes: 6 cups

A reduction of red wine and balsamic vinegar makes a wonderful not-too-sweet dressing for fruit. For a change, add crunch by sprinkling a few caramelized walnuts or pecans on the fruit just before serving.

4 cups strawberries, washed, hulled and halved
2 cups seedless black or red grapes, halved
3/4 cup balsamic vinegar
1/4 cup dry red wine
1/4 cup granulated sugar
pinch of salt
1 tbs. fresh lemon juice
1 tbs. lemon zest
4 whole cloves
1/3 tsp. pure vanilla extract

Combine strawberries and grapes in serving bowl. Cover and refrigerate while preparing dressing.

In a small, non-reactive saucepan, cook vinegar, red wine, sugar and salt on medium-high heat for about 15 minutes. This mixture will reduce to a syrupy consistency. Add lemon juice, lemon zest and cloves and cook for 1 to 2 minutes longer. Remove from heat, stir in vanilla and strain mixture through a sieve. Allow sauce to cool to room temperature. Pour this sauce over fruit and chill until ready to serve. Serve within 3 to 4 hours for best results

Note: Aluminum, copper and cast iron are reactive materials. Stainless steel, glass and nonstick are non-reactive.

BERRY, TURKEY AND CASHEW SALAD

This colorful salad is healthy and versatile. Cooked chicken can be substituted for the turkey and tropical fruit like papaya or mango can be added for a change. Toasted macadamia nuts can also be used in place of cashews.

4 cups mixed greens
1½ cups cubed cooked turkey
1¼ cup sliced strawberries, washed and hulled
2 kiwis, peeled and sliced
⅔ cup dry-roasted, salted cashews
¼ cup chopped green onions
2 tbs. toasted sesame seeds

SESAME-LEMON DRESSING

¼ cup olive oil
¼ cup honey
¼ cup fresh lemon juice
1 tbs. sesame oil
salt and black pepper to taste

Divide mixed greens between 4 plates. Artfully arrange turkey, strawberries, kiwis and cashews over greens and sprinkle with green onions and sesame seeds.

In a food processor or blender, combine dressing ingredients and pour over salad just before serving.

SPINACH, BACON AND STRAWBERRY SALAD

This simple salad is a summertime favorite and a refreshing starter dish. Variations on this salad could be the addition of caramelized pecans, sautéed sweet onions or toasted almonds.

8 cups fresh spinach leaves, washed and dried
1 cup sliced fresh strawberries, washed and hulled
1 small red onion, very thinly sliced
8 slices bacon or prosciutto, cooked and diced
2 tbs. toasted pine nuts or sesame seeds

HONEY-MUSTARD DRESSING

3 tbs. rice wine vinegar
3 tbs. balsamic vinegar
2 tbs. honey
1 tbs. Dijon mustard
salt and black pepper to taste

Remove stems from washed spinach and divide between 4 salad plates. Sprinkle strawberries, onions, bacon and pine nuts (or sesame seeds) over spinach.

With a food processor or blender, combine all dressing ingredients, then sample and adjust to your personal taste. Drizzle dressing over salad just before serving.

ORANGE BERRY SOUP

Servings: 4

Oranges and strawberries make a great combination. I like to serve this soup with moist bran muffins or buttered crumpets. Frozen strawberries can be substituted in this recipe.

1 lb. coarsely chopped fresh strawberries, washed and hulled
1½ cups orange juice, freshly squeezed preferred
⅓ cup sugar
2 tbs. fresh lime juice
1 tsp. grated fresh ginger
dollop of sweetened whipped cream for garnish, optional

Place all ingredients in a food processor workbowl or blender container and blend until smooth. Taste and add more lime juice or sugar if desired.

PORK ROAST WITH CUMIN BERRY SAUCE

Servings: 4

This sauce would also work with poultry and game meats.

one 3 lb. pork loin roast
3 garlic cloves
salt and black pepper to taste
1 cup sliced fresh strawberries

½ cup strawberry jam
¼ cup boysenberry or
   marionberry jam
⅓ cup raspberry jam
1 tsp. ground cumin

Preheat oven to 350°. Peel garlic cloves and cut into slivers. Pierce pork roast several times with the point of a knife and stuff garlic slivers in the holes. Sprinkle entire roast with salt and pepper. Place roast in baking dish and cook for about 1 hour, until thermometer reads at least 160°. Pork should be slightly pink inside. Remove roast from oven and allow meat to stand for 15 minutes before slicing.

In a medium saucepan, stir together fresh strawberries, three jams and cumin, heat mixture on medium until strawberries are tender. Slice roast and serve with warm sauce.

CORNISH HENS IN MADEIRA BERRY SAUCE

Servings: 2–4

Madeira wine counterbalances the sweetness of strawberries. Add the strawberries at the end of the cooking process to help retain color and shape.

2 Cornish game hens, about
  1–1¼ lb. each
black pepper to taste
8 slices of bacon
1½ tbs. olive oil
1½ tbs. butter
½ cup sliced shallots
2 tsp. fresh thyme leaves or

¾ tsp. dried
2 tsp. fresh rosemary leaves or
  ¾ tsp. dried and ground
⅔ cup Madeira wine
¾ cup chicken broth
1 cup sliced fresh strawberries,
  washed and hulled

Wash, pat dry and split Cornish hens down the back. Place game hens in baking dish, skin side up. Sprinkle hens with black pepper and cover each hen with 4 slices of bacon. Bake in a 400° oven for 15 minutes; reduce heat to 350° and bake for an additional 20 to 25 minutes. Remove from oven, remove bacon, if desired, and cover with aluminum to keep warm.

While the birds are cooking, heat olive oil and butter in a medium non-reactive saucepan. Sauté shallots for about 2 minutes, until tender, then add thyme, rosemary, Madeira and chicken broth. Bring sauce to a boil over high heat and cook for about 2 to 3 minutes, until slightly reduced. Add strawberries and reduce heat to medium. Cook until berries are just tender. Taste and adjust seasonings. Pour sauce over hens and serve immediately.

TUNA WITH BERRY SALSA

Servings: 4

Fresh tuna is marinated then broiled and served with a fresh strawberry and bell pepper salsa. This salsa recipe also goes well with poultry dishes.

4 tbs. chopped basil leaves
2/3 cup olive oil
2 tbs. balsamic vinegar
3 tbs. water
4 tsp. soy sauce

1/2 tsp. black pepper
1/2 tsp. sugar
1/4 tsp. salt
4 pc. tuna, about 1 1/2–2 lb.

Place all ingredients except tuna in a food processor workbowl or blender container and process until well blended. Lay tuna (single layer) in a dish and pour on marinade. Cover with plastic wrap and marinate for at least 4 hours, turning tuna after 2 hours. Broil or barbecue tuna until charbroiled on the outside and slightly pink in the center, about 3 minutes per side. Serve immediately with *Berry Salsa*.

BERRY SALSA

This salsa goes well with fish and poultry. You can also serve this as a dip by processing the ingredients with a food processor until finely chopped. Use tortilla chips or toasted bread rounds as an accompaniment.

1½ cups sliced strawberries, washed and hulled
½ red bell pepper, seeded and cut into long, thin strips
½ yellow bell pepper, seeded and cut into long, thin strips
½ green bell pepper, seeded and cut into long, thin strips
½ red onion, very thinly sliced
⅓ cup finely chopped cilantro
⅓ cup orange juice
3 tbs. olive oil
2–3 tbs. fresh lime juice
salt and black pepper to taste
1 jalapeño pepper, seeded and minced, optional

Simply mix all the ingredients together in a bowl, then taste and adjust seasonings. If desired, add minced jalapeño.

PORK WITH STRAWBERRY LYCHEE SAUCE

Servings: 4

I frequently use pork tenderloin because it is the ideal meat for a quick meal. Lychees are sweet tropical fruit that have the consistency similar to grapes. They are now available in most supermarkets. Serve with plain rice or rice pilaf.

1–1½ lb. pork tenderloin
salt and black pepper to taste
1 tbs. olive oil
2 tbs. butter
½ cup Madeira wine
¾ cup lychees, drained and halved
¾ cup strawberries, washed and hulled
1 tbs. sugar

Cut pork tenderloin into round medallions about ½-inch thick and season with salt and pepper. Heat olive oil and butter in a skillet on medium-high heat and quickly sauté meat until browned on both sides. Cook until pink is just barely cooked out of the meat. Remove medallions from pan and keep warm, wrapped in aluminum.

Deglaze pan by adding Madeira wine and stirring up the brown bits. Add remaining ingredients, quartering strawberries if large or halving berries if small. Simmer for 1 to 2 minutes until strawberries are slightly cooked. Add pork back to the pan. Taste and adjust seasonings. Serve immediately.

Note: If you are not a fan of lychees, simply increase the quantity of strawberries or use seedless green grapes.

LAMB WITH STRAWBERRY MINT SAUCE

Servings: 8

This Strawberry Mint Sauce *can be served savory or sweet. Heat when serving with cooked meat but serve chilled as a topping for desserts. This is particularly good with lemon-flavored desserts.*

one 4–5 lb. boneless leg of lamb
4–5 garlic cloves, peeled
1¼ tbs. salt
2½ tbs. chopped fresh rosemary

½ tsp. black pepper
drizzle of olive oil
¼ cup beef broth
salt and pepper to taste

Trim most of the fat off lamb. Score lamb in a criss-cross pattern to ensure rub fully flavors meat. Mash garlic and salt together into a paste and add chopped rosemary and pepper. Spread rub all over lamb. Drizzle olive oil in a roasting pan and set lamb in pan. Allow lamb to set at room temperature for 30 minutes before roasting.

Heat oven to 350°. Place a thermometer into lamb and bake until it registers 130°, about 1¼ hours. Remove lamb from oven and let stand for 20 minutes before carving. Internal temperature will rise to about 140°. Meanwhile, heat roasting pan with meat juices on top of the stove on high heat. Pour beef broth into roasting pan and stir to scrape up brown bits. Taste and determine if you wish to add salt and pepper. Pour this over sliced lamb and serve *Strawberry Mint Sauce* on the side.

STRAWBERRY MINT SAUCE

½ cup firmly packed fresh mint leaves
¼ cup sugar
1 pint strawberries, washed, hulled and halved
½ cup water
a few drops of lemon juice, optional

Place mint leaves on a cutting board and sprinkle sugar over. Finely chop mint and sugar together. Transfer sugared mint to a food processor workbowl or blender container; add strawberries and water and process into a purée. Taste and determine if you wish to add some lemon juice to "sparkle" the flavor. Place mixture in a saucepan and just barely heat to warm. Serve with roasted lamb.

STRAWBERRY CREAM CAKE

Servings: 10–12

The frosting is what makes this cake so phenomenal! It is light and fluffy and can be used with any flavor of cake.

1 pkg. white cake mix
one 10 oz. pkg. frozen strawberries, partially thawed
4 eggs
one 3 oz. pkg. strawberry gelatin
$\frac{1}{2}$ cup vegetable oil
$\frac{1}{4}$ cup hot water

In a bowl, combine all ingredients and pour into two 9-inch pans lined with brown paper or parchment and lightly buttered. Bake at 350° for 25 to 30 minutes. Allow cake to cool thoroughly before frosting.

WHIPPED CREAM FROSTING

1/2 cup butter, softened
8 oz. cream cheese, softened
1 cup powdered sugar
1 tsp. pure vanilla extract

pinch of salt
2 cups heavy cream
2 cups fresh strawberries

In a large bowl, beat butter and cream cheese together until creamy. Add powdered sugar, vanilla and salt and beat until mixed. Add heavy cream and beat until frosting thickens to spreading consistency.

Cut fresh strawberries into slices, leaving 1 whole for the center. Spread part of the frosting between the layers and use half of the strawberries between layers. Spread a little more frosting over strawberries to hold layers together. Cover cake with remaining frosting. Place whole strawberry in center of cake top and then place sliced strawberries upright in concentric circles around top of cake.

HEARTS OF CREAM
WITH STRAWBERRY SAUCE

Servings: 6

This dessert is traditionally served on Valentine's Day but it can be served in any season because this recipe uses frozen strawberries. Garnish with mint leaves and flowers, if desired.

2 envelopes unflavored gelatin
1/4 cup cold water
1 pint whipping cream
1 cup sugar
2 cups sour cream
1 tsp. pure vanilla extract

In a small bowl, combine gelatin and cold water and let sit for about 5 minutes, until softened.

In a large saucepan, heat cream, sugar and gelatin over low heat until gelatin is completely dissolved, whisking as needed. Remove from heat and allow mixture to cool. Fold sour cream and vanilla into cooled gelatin mixture. Spray a 5 to 6 cup mold or individual molds with a cooking spray and pour in cream mixture. Refrigerate for at least 4 hours or overnight. Serve with *Strawberry Sauce*.

STRAWBERRY SAUCE
two 10 oz. pkg. frozen strawberries, thawed
sugar to taste
1 tsp. orange zest
1 dash orange liqueur, or to taste if desired

In a food processor workbowl or blender container, purée all ingredients and adjust sugar to your taste. Unmold hearts of cream and pour sauce on top.

COCONUT AND STRAWBERRY CREAM

Servings: 4

This quick dessert is refreshing and simple. For a change, you can use a combination of berries.

2 cups sliced strawberries, washed and hulled
1/2 cup sweetened condensed milk
1/4 tsp. salt
1 tbs. fresh lemon juice
3/4 cup pineapple juice
1 cup shredded coconut

Place sliced berries in glass pie pan or medium-sized dish. In a mixer, beat sweetened condensed milk, salt, lemon juice and pineapple together until fluffy. Spread this mixture over berries and refrigerate for at least 2 hours. Toast coconut under broiler until brown and sprinkle over mixture just before serving.

STRATBERRY TREE

Servings: 12

This technique can be used as a centerpiece to a fruit tray or served by itself with a flavored yogurt, fruit dipping sauce or melted chocolate in a fondue pot.

1 large whole pineapple with fresh looking leaves
2 pints fresh strawberries with stems attached
red frilled toothpicks
garnish with flowers

Using scissors, trim off any wilted leaves on top of the pineapple, cutting at an angle to create a pointed leaf. Stick a frilled toothpick through the bottom of a strawberry and attach it to pineapple, with stem side against pineapple.

Fill in berries side-by-side in concentric circles around pineapple, completely covering pineapple, except for the leaves. Garnish leaves and base of pineapple with flowers.

MELON MELANGE

This is a refreshing summer dessert for the adult palate. A variety of melon balls are soaked in a strawberry and Grand Marnier sauce.

6 cups melon balls (cantaloupe, honeydew, and crenshaw and/or
   casaba melon)
1–4 tbs. sugar, to taste
1–3 tsp. fresh lemon juice, to taste
4 cups fresh strawberries
3/4 cup sugar
1/2 cup red currant jelly
2 tbs. Grand Marnier liqueur
2 tbs. Midori (melon liqueur) or Kirsch, optional

Use a combination of melons of choice. Sprinkle melon balls with sugar and lemon juice to taste (depending on the sweetness of the melons). Keep chilled until ready to serve.

Reserve a few strawberries for garnish. Wash, hull and quarter remaining strawberries. Place strawberries, sugar, red currant jelly and Grand Marnier in a food processor workbowl or blender container and process until puréed. Taste and determine if you wish to add the Midori or Kirsch liqueur. Chill until ready to serve. Pour strawberry purée over melon balls just before serving. Garnish with the reserved whole strawberries.

ITALIAN BERRIES

Servings: 4–6

This delightful, simple dessert is served over vanilla ice cream. Do not try to substitute any other kind of vinegar—balsamic is a must!

⅓ cup balsamic vinegar
1 tbs. granulated sugar
½ tsp. fresh lemon juice
3 pts. strawberries

1 cup light brown sugar
pinch of black pepper
½ gal. vanilla ice cream

In a small saucepan, combine vinegar, granulated sugar and lemon juice and stir over medium heat until reduced in half. Allow this mixture to cool.

Wash, hull and slice strawberries. Sprinkle berries with brown sugar and allow the mixture to macerate (juice exudes from berries) for about 15 minutes. Sprinkle with a little black pepper. Pour cooled vinegar mixture over berries and serve over ice cream.

STRAWBERRY TOPPING

Serve this wonderful topping over cheesecake, angel food cake, pound cake or ice cream.

2 lb. sliced strawberries, washed and hulled
⅓–½ cup sugar, depending on sweetness of berries
1 pinch salt
1 cup strawberry jam
2 tbs. fresh lemon juice

In a bowl, combine strawberries, sugar and salt and allow mixture to sit for about 30 minutes to release juice from berries. In a food processor or blender, process jam and lemon juice until smooth and transfer to a small saucepan. Cook jam mixture on medium for 3 to 4 minutes, until jam begins to darken. Pour jam mixture over berries, stir and allow mixture to cool. Cover and refrigerate until ready to serve.

RHUBARB-STRAWBERRY FOOL

Fool is a dessert made of stewed or puréed fruit which is served chilled with sweetened whipped cream. I like to layer the fruit and cream "parfait-style" in fluted glasses to enhance the visual appeal.

1 lb. rhubarb
$\frac{1}{3}$ cup orange juice
$\frac{3}{4}$ cup sugar
pinch of salt
2 pts. strawberries, washed, hulled, quartered
2 cups heavy cream
$\frac{1}{3}$ cup sugar
$\frac{1}{2}$ tsp. pure vanilla extract
whole strawberries for garnish

Trim ends of rhubarb and soak in cold water for 15 to 20 minutes. Cut rhubarb into $\frac{1}{2}$-inch pieces.

Meanwhile, in a non-reactive, medium saucepan, bring orange juice, sugar and salt to a boil. Add rhubarb and strawberries. Reduce heat to medium-low and cook, stirring occasionally, for about 8 to 10 minutes, until rhubarb is tender. *Note: avoid over-stirring rhubarb—it will take on a mushy consistency.* Transfer ingredients to a glass bowl, cover and refrigerate until ready to assemble.

Whip heavy cream with ⅓ cup sugar and vanilla until thick and mixture forms soft peaks.

Serve chilled cooked fruit in individual bowls with a large dollop of flavored whipped cream and garnish with a fresh strawberry. Or serve as a parfait: spoon about ¼ cup of fruit into bottom of glass, add a dollop of whipped cream and repeat the procedure. Garnish with a fresh strawberry.

HAZELNUT DIPPED STRAWBERRIES

Makes: about. 24

Semi-sweet or milk chocolate can be substituted for white chocolate and almonds or macadamia nuts can be used in place of hazelnuts.

1½ cups hazelnuts, without skins
one 12 oz. pkg. white chocolate chips or chocolate of choice
1 pint fresh strawberries, with stems

Spread hazelnuts on a cookie sheet and place under broiler until nuts begin to brown. Stir nuts lightly and continue to broil until nuts are browned all over. Remove from oven and crush nuts with a rolling pin.

Melt chocolate chips either by double boiler or microwave, according to package instructions. Holding strawberry by the stem, dip about ¾ ways up in melted chocolate then roll in crushed toasted nuts. Lay a piece of waxed paper on a cookie sheet and place coated strawberries on wax paper. Chill berries in refrigerator for about 10 to 15 minutes to harden chocolate.

CREAMY STRAWBERRY FONDUE

Servings 4–6

Strawberries and cream cheese are a winning combination. Usually, I serve this with pound cake, angel food cubes or even crisp cookies. But consider serving a small platter of fruits for dipping.

8 oz. cream cheese, softened
2 tbs. brandy, Amaretto or liqueur of choice
one 10 oz. pkg. frozen strawberries, thawed
sugar to taste

In a small saucepan, heat cream cheese and brandy or liqueur over medium heat and stir to combine. Finely chop strawberries and stir into cream cheese mixture. Taste and determine how much sugar you wish to add. Keep warm in a fondue pot.

EXTREME STRAWBERRY ICE CREAM

Makes: 1 gallon

Fresh berries make the best ice cream. If you want to take it to the next level of extreme, serve with Strawberry Topping, *page 59.*

3 lb. sliced fresh strawberries, washed and hulled
1 cup sugar
2 tbs. fresh lemon juice
4 large eggs, beaten
two 14 oz. cans sweetened condensed milk
$\frac{1}{2}$ cup granulated sugar
$\frac{1}{3}$ cup light brown sugar
4 cups heavy whipping cream
4 cups half-and-half
$\frac{1}{2}$ tsp. salt
4 tbs. pure vanilla extract or 2 vanilla beans, split and scraped

In a large bowl, combine strawberries, sugar and lemon juice and allow berries to macerate (exude juice) for about 1 hour.

Mix remaining ingredients together and refrigerate until ready to use. Transfer strawberry mixture to a large saucepan, heat to a boil then reduce heat to simmer and cook for 5 minutes to soften berries.

Remove pan from heat and allow to cool. Using a food processor or blender, process strawberries until finely chopped. Stir strawberry mixture into chilled egg and cream mixture and freeze according to ice cream freezer machine instructions.

RAINBOW STRAWBERRY BOMBE

Servings: 8–10

Use either a large decorative mold or serving bowl to freeze this delicious concoction. Slice the bombe into wedges and serve in a bed of Strawberry Sauce, *page 53.*

3 quarts ice cream of choice (i.e. strawberry, vanilla and chocolate)
two 10 oz. pkg. frozen strawberries or 2 cups fresh sliced strawberries
¼ cup orange or strawberry liqueur or liqueur of choice
additional sugar to taste
1 whole strawberry and sprig of mint for garnish

Chill the mold or serving bowl before packing. Soften the first quart of ice cream and smooth evenly into the bottom third of mold. Be sure to pack ice cream firmly so that no air spaces remain. Place in freezer until firm. Repeat this procedure with the two remaining flavors until mold is filled.

Cover the surface with a plastic wrap and freeze for at least 6 hours. Remove from freezer 30 minutes before serving.

HINTS

1. Do not set directly on freezer shelf (place on a package).
2. Bombes are best if used within 24 hours of making.
3. To unmold, run cool water over the mold briefly and serve on a chilled platter.

To make sauce, combine frozen or fresh strawberries in a food processor workbowl or blender container with liqueur of choice. Taste and determine if you wish to add a little sugar to sweeten the sauce. Spoon sauce onto serving plate and place a slice of bombe on top. Garnish with whole strawberry and mint.

RED, WHITE AND BLUE PHYLLO TARTLETS

Phyllo dough creates a quick flaky crust that can be used for sweet desserts or savory appetizers.

8 sheets phyllo dough
1/2 cup butter, melted
8 oz. cream cheese, softened
1/3 cup powdered sugar
1 1/2 tbs. grated orange zest
fresh strawberries, whole or sliced
fresh blueberries
1/2 cup apricot jam for glaze, optional

Preheat oven to 375°. Lightly brush phyllo sheets with butter and stack four sheets high. Cut stack into 3 inch squares and place in miniature muffin tins. Bake for about 10 minutes, until tartlets turn golden.

Allow tartlets to cool before filling.

In a small bowl, combine cream cheese, sugar and orange zest together until smooth. Divide this filling between tartlets and top with a fresh strawberry and a few blueberries.

If desired, heat apricot jam in a small saucepan on medium and brush on fruit. This helps to retain the freshness of the fruit and adds a little sweetness to the tartlet.

SHORTCAKE

This recipe is slightly different from the traditional shortcake due to the addition of cream cheese and buttermilk. Serve with sweetened sliced strawberries and a large dollop of sweetened whipped cream flavored with a little vanilla extract.

2½ cups all-purpose flour
⅓ cup sugar
4 tsp. baking powder
1 tsp. baking soda
1 tsp. salt
½ cup cold butter
8 oz. cold cream cheese
¾ cup buttermilk
a little buttermilk and coarse sugar for sprinkling

Preheat oven to 450°. Using a food processor, process flour, sugar, baking powder, baking soda, and salt together until mixed. Cut up butter into pieces and process until butter is the size of peas. Then cut up cream cheese, add to processor and process until cream cheese is the size of peas. Add buttermilk and pulse until dough comes together.

Flour a board, roll out dough to about 1/2-inch thick and cut into rounds. Place rounds on cookie sheet, brush with a little buttermilk and sprinkle with coarse sugar, such as demerara sugar. Bake for 15 minutes or until golden brown.

STRAWBERRY SORBET

Servings: 6

Sorbet is a sweetened frozen fruit concoction that is made without cream. If you do not have an ice cream machine, this recipe can be frozen in a 9-x-13-inch pan. But remove pan from the freezer 15 minutes before serving.

2 cups water
1 cup sugar
1 qt. fresh strawberries, washed, hulled and halved
$\frac{1}{3}$ cup lemon juice
$\frac{1}{3}$ cup orange juice
$\frac{1}{2}$–1 cup finely chopped strawberries to add texture, optional

In a heavy saucepan, heat water and sugar on high heat until sugar dissolves, about 5 minutes. Do not stir mixture: simply swirl pan over heat to avoid crystallizing sugar.

Purée strawberries in food processor or blender; add lemon juice and orange juice and blend to mix. Remove sugar syrup from heat and stir in strawberry mixture. At this point, determine if you wish to add chopped strawberries for texture.

Cover and refrigerate for 2 hours before placing in an ice cream machine. Process sorbet according to ice cream machine manufacturer's instructions.

Note: If freezing in a 9-x-13-inch pan, freeze for approximately 6 hours, stirring with a fork every hour. Cover and freeze sorbet in an airtight container.

SWEET AND SOUR STRAWBERRIES

This is a quick and simple "adult" recipe for dessert. Only fresh berries will work and the amount of sugar is determined by the sweetness of the strawberries.

4 cups sliced fresh strawberries
Sparkling Gamay Beaujolais wine, to taste
4 dollops of sour cream
4–8 tbs. brown sugar (start with 4 tbs. and increase to taste)

Place 1 cup each of sliced strawberries in 4 individual bowls. Pour enough sparkling Gamay Beaujolais to just moisten berries. Top with sour cream and sprinkle with brown sugar.

Note: serve with Sparkling Gamay Beaujolais alongside if desired.

INDEX